Cowpunchers, Sheep Herders, and Plain Pig Farmers

WILD WEST LIMERICKS

By Gwen Petersen
and Jeane Rhodes

ILLUSTRATED BY
ALAN RHODES

Distributed by

Laffing Cow Press
PO Box 3106
Cheyenne, WY 82003
(800) 722-6932

Second Printing, 1991

Library of Congress Catalog Card Number: 85-90342
ISBN 0-934318-57-3

CONTENTS

Introduction:

The lack of wild and woolly western limericks has long been a gap in Montana's cultural landscape.

Gwen Petersen and Jeane Rhodes have corrected that oversight. It is said that people who write, read, or recite limericks have either a skewed sense of reality or a kinship with Shakespeare.

One of these authors is askew and the other bears watching.

Two women who live in the West
Found nary a verse that expressed
The West as they knew it—
With grit to get through it—
And decided to rise to the test.

Now limericks must stick to the rules
And not merely wander like mules,
So here Jeane and Gwen
Both wielded a pen
And lassoed these wild Western jewels.

RANCHIN' 'N WRANGLERS

COWGIRLS AND COWBOYS

Cowgirls maintain an exterior
Pretending they're really inferior;
But each of them knows,
From her head to her toes,
Her construction is vastly superior.

A cowgirl knows just what she shouldn't do,
And several things that she wouldn't do,
But, by God, to her credit
Though she never has said it,
There really ain't much that she couldn't do.

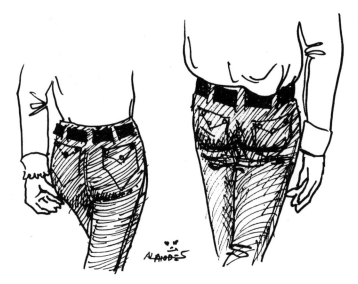

If a cowgirl gets dressy, she smothers,
Cause ruffles and heels are for others;
To cope with cow creatures,
Tight pants are the features,
So cowgirls dress just like their brothers.

No women, not grannies, not lasses—
Nor any such downtrodden classes,
Are allowed in corrals—
Not no kind of gals—
Just wait until ERA passes.

The cowgirl who's out on the tractor
Is happy except for one factor;
When every last bump
Meets up with her rump,
She's certain that someone has smacked her.

The hay hand fell off of his stack
And struck with a horrible whack.
But his wife braved the fescue
To come to his rescue.
And toted him home in a sack.

Cowboys are born without diapers,
Midst sagebrush and cactus and vipers,
So they have to be tough,
Which may be enough
To make them the world's loudest gripers.

A cowboy has legs just like wickets,
And thinks that they're really the tickets!
But folks from the city
Regard him with pity—
They think he's a victim of rickets.

A cowboy out riding the range
Discovered a thing rather strange,
A bald headed girl
With nary a curl
Who'd lost all her hair from the mange.

Oh, pity the cowboy who's coming
From night-herding duty that's numbing,
Through cowpies quite dense
Deposited thence
By cattle with very loose plumbing.

The cowboy shook out a big loop
And snared the mean bull with a whoop.
He took in the slack
And snap went his back...
He's known around town as "Ol' Stoop".

JES DON'T STEP IN IT!

A cowboy intent on his toil
Must heed nature's call lest he spoil,
So he piles off his horse
And does something quite coarse;
He knows it enriches the soil.

9

For riding way out on the prairie
The facilities tend to be airy,
You can bet from the spot
Where you've chosen to squat,
That your profile will show—so don't tarry.

To hear some range-riders talk,
And brag on their numerous stock,
The most fun alive
Is a long cattle drive,
But cattle don't drive, they just walk.

If a robber says, "This is a stick-up!
Give me your hoss or your pick-up!"
Unless he's a saint,
Clyde'll part with ol' Paint
Without even so much as a hiccup.

When riding a bucker take pains
To keep careful hold of the reins,
Or else try some glue
Twixt the saddle and you
Lest the maverick scatter your brains.

A furious cowboy named Clyde,
Rode madly across the divide,
He continued down hill
At the same pace until
He fell in the ocean and died.

While rocking along at a lope
His horse bucked him off on a slope;
It wounded his pride
So now, for a ride,
Clyde ties himself on with a rope.

When Clyde hunkered down on his heels,
He suddenly broke out in squeals;
The spurs he'd forgotten
Went clean through his bottom—
He stands now when taking his meals.

Old Clyde who had plenty of brass
Rode madly up over the pass,
Intending to murder
That stinkin' sheepherder
Whose sheep had grazed off all his grass.

Handsome and tall and mustached,
Clyde fell off his cayuse and mashed
His favorite part,
And I don't mean his heart,
Cause the heartless don't feel so abashed.

Oh Clyde he got hung in a wire gate
And fervently cussed at his dire fate;
His words, so heartfelt,
Caused the wire to melt,
And he got home in time to retire, late.

The lodgings of cowboys are humble,
They live in a terrible jumble;
But they thrive on the dirt,
And unless they get hurt,
Old cowboys don't die, they just crumble.

Though little in life is for sure,
Three things on the ranch will endure—
Sticky mud to your thighs,
Ugly bugs every size,
And a steady supply of manure.

SHEEPHERDERS AND PIG FARMERS

A sheepherder's wagon is small,
Just a bunk and a stove and a wall.
He can cook and can sleep
And can tend to his sheep,
But overnight guests? Not at all.

A sheepherder fat as a coot
Piled stones up to mark out his route.
The stones started joggin',
And fell on his noggin'
And now he is crazy to boot.

A sheepherder known as Good Sam
Fell flat on a sweet little lamb.
"Oh, golly," he said
"I've killed it plumb dead,
And frankly, I don't give a damn."

The sow toppled over the cream,
And lay in the widening stream;
Said she, "It's my duty
To care for my beauty,
To look like Miss Piggy's my dream."

" TRUSSED ME ! "

Oinked the boar, "This I know will concern ya,
But since I've developed a hernia,
I'm so dad-blamed sore
I can no longer bore,
So I'm forced at this moment to spurn ya."

There was an old sow in the barn
Had 23 piglets, by darn.
"I curse that old boar,"
Said she with a roar,
"Oh, when will ever I larn!"

A sow sidled up to the wagon
Where the farmer spilled booze from his flagon.
She lapped up the liquid
Like any good pig would,
And both of them got quite a jag on.

OUTHOUSES AND COWS

Cows round the outhouse—what din!
Their mooing gets under my skin;
I'll sit here, no doubt,
Afraid to step out,
For fear of what I will step <u>in.</u>

Cows round the outhouse are nosy
Their moos make you feel warm and cozy
They graze and they share
What is fertilized there
While depositing many a posy.

The view from the outhouse was dandy,
But the paper was No. 2 sandy;
Said the cowboy, "Don't grieve,
I'll wipe on my sleeve,
Which is softer, but somewhat unhandy."

CRITTERS 'N CUSSIN'

COWS, CALVES, BULLS 'N STEERS

A bull calf who wasn't too wary yet
Got caught in the loop of a lariat;
    Ignoring his squalls,
    They cut off his balls—
Of offspring he hasn't a nary yet.

Alas, since early this morning,
The steers have lost all their adorning;
    They went through the chute,
    Pausing en route,
For branding, castrating, dehorning.

The brockle-faced cow had a fit
When her calf caught hold of a tit.
    "Oh, surely this tot'll
    Survive on the bottle,"
Said she, "not on me, cause I quit!"

Old Bessie, the milk cow said, "Ow,"
When bit on the tit by a sow.
    With her trusty hind foot
    She took aim and put
That pig out of reach of the chow.

HORSES, MULES 'N DONKEYS

Beware of that friendly fast talker
Who claims his horse's smooth as a rocker,
One thing you can bet
If you ride on his pet,
You'll be glad to once more be a walker.

Lone Ranger, you're selfish as sin, so
Your bias we'll have to look into—
For Silver, of course, is
The Rolls Royce of horses,
While Tonto gets only a Pinto.

A wild horse just in from the range
Considers all humans as strange;
If anyone mounts him,
The mustang discounts him
And hands back his teeth as exchange.

A tired old cowhorse named Unc
Was replaced by a bike with more spunk;
One day with a squall,
To the wonder of all,
He reduced his replacement to junk.

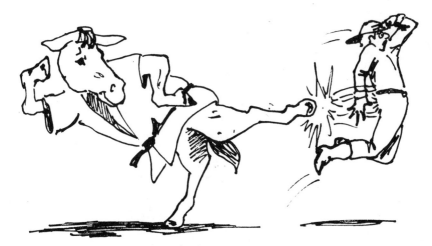

Mules can be meaner than sin.
They really get under your skin.
If you dare turn your back,
They are sure to attack.
And kick you where you have just been.

There once was an albino donkey,
So his cohorts all labelled him, "Honkey"
Which would be a pity,
But he strayed to the city
Where he brays in a smart honkey-tonkey.

EWES, LAMBS 'N COYOTES

A sheep is a cute woolly creature
Whose coat is its very best feature;
It feels so forlorn
Whenever it's shorn
That it won't even bleat to greet yer.

A matronly sheep named Maude Dupets
Gave birth to a set of quadruplets.
"Oh, what shall I do?"
Cried the motherly ewe,
"My faucets come only in two sets!"

The coyote said, "Ain't I cute?"
As he bit off a lamb's little snoot.
But the herder said, "You're
Cuter when fewer.
To endanger your species, I'll shoot."

A coyote pursuing a hunch
Spotted some sheep in a bunch.
"Oh, yum," he exclaimed,
As he wounded and maimed,
"I'll have a sheep sandwich for lunch."

A coyote crept up on a sheep
And captured her lamb with a leap;
"Oh, Lambie, don't cry,"
Said the ewe with a sigh,
"You're part of the coyote's upkeep."

VARIOUS VORACIOUS VARMINTS

A heel fly badly off course
Found the nose of a lone cowboy's horse;
The horse took offence
And hither and hence
Flew the cowboy with words rather coarse.

The big irrigator went wham!
His shovel collapsed on the dam.
He jumped in the ditch,
"You son-of-a-bitch!"
He cried; now the beaver is Spam.

Joe said to the snake, "You're my enem-
y, but I'm not afraid of your venom."
What happened to Joe
We really don't know,
But the snake is now wearing blue denim.

A magpie flew off with some eggs
While the farmer chased just on his legs,
But his old equalizer
Showed which one was wiser
And left that old magpie in dregs.

"Quit stealing my eggs, you magpie!"
Said the ranch gal with blood in her eye.
"Ha, you can't catch me,"
Said the bird in great glee.
So she shot him rather than try.

The prairie dog pops from his burrow
And sights a convenient furrow;
It's green and it's sprouting,
So he plans an outing—
At chewing it up he'll be thorough.

Gophers look cutsie and charming
But some of their ways are alarming.
For one, they'll devour
Each leaf, stalk and flower
Of whatever crop you are farming.

Snakes slither out after sunrise
To wait till the dewy wet soil dries.
They coil in a pile
And wait with a smile,
To scare you right out of your levis.

SPORTIN' 'N SPIRITS

COURTING

A cowboy both silent and shy
Fell in love with a girl on the sly.
But he wouldn't shout
So she never found out,
And she married a talkative guy.

The cowboy went shyly a-courting
A maiden they told him was sporting.
But when she resisted,
His tongue became twisted.
The outcome is not worth reporting.

"I'll do the ropin' and tyin'
While you do the fetchin' and fryin',"
He said, waxing glib,
But she was a lib,
So the cowboy's still single and tryin'.

A dashing young cowgirl named Nancy
Saw a cowboy she really could fancy;
    She sneaked up beside him,
    And roped him and tied him,
Cuz running 'em loose can be chancy.

A macho young farmer named Ed
Could pitch bales of hay overhead;
    But he found out one day
    Better uses for hay—
Now it's woo that he pitches instead.

A sheepherder come into cash
Went searching for females with dash;
But reeking so badly
That one told him sadly
His air was more sheep than panache.

LOLLYGAGGING

Oh, Marlboro Man, or Lone Ranger,
Or Redford, or you, Handsome Stranger,
To lift up your mask
Is all that I ask,
And roll you around in the manger.

Lone Ranger said, "Silver, you're true blue.
I'll live with nobody but you."
And that's why the lasses
Exclaim as he passes,
"Who WAS that masked man—Phe-eww!"

A cowboy of dashing and splendor
Appeals to the feminine gender,
But somehow he's tough
Toward females and fluff,
Though to horses and cows he is tender.

A seven foot tall lady angler
Fell in love with a bucking horse wrangler.
They attempted to court
But the bunk was so short,
In the morning they couldn't untangler.

A cowboy who seems to be prancing,
Retreating, then later advancing,
As though in some pain—
I'd like to explain,
It's just his idea of dancing.

A cowboy rode fast round a pasture
Pursuing a girl who ran faster,
She shouted, "You dope,
You haven't a hope,
I'm in love with a whistling bull wrassler!"

Calamity Jane had such fun,
As she raised hell in town with her gun,
But she met with Wild Bill
Before trying the Pill,
And now she is raising a son.

The cowpoke a wife did acquire,
Expecting to sit by the fire.
But he's left his abode
For a life on the road
Cause wifey's a champion goat-tyer.

TIPPLING

A cowboy is fond of his whiskey
It makes him ferociously frisky,
So, heed my advice,
Don't go with one twice,
Cuz once is sufficiently risky.

Cowboys, we know, take to drinkin'
And turn wobbly legged and stinkin',
Then set out with pals
To lasso some gals,
But can't do much other than winkin".

A well-oiled cowboy named Durbin
Found falling in ditches disturbin',
He lay there and wallowed,
And gasped as he swallowed,
"This ditch water sure needs some bourbon!"

The boys in the bunkhouse play gin
With anyone wandering in,
But if they should lose,
They go out and booze—
The same thing they do if they win.

A dance in the schoolhouse is fun
But the cowboys all fade one by one.
They booze every chance
To get courage to dance—
But boozing is all they get done.

DOIN'S 'N DUDS

HATS, BRITCHES, BOOTS, SPURS 'N CHAPS

A cowboy hat's made with great pains
To guard him from sunshine and rains,
With a wide band for sweat
So his eyes don't get wet
And a crown that's too big for his brains.

Cowboys wear odd leather chaps
Constructed with generous gaps;
The reason you see,
Is so they can pee
Without inundating their laps.

The cowboy wore jeans very tight
As he ventured out into the night;
He couldn't help sneezing
And ended up freezing
The part of him seeing the light.

The cowboy wore spurs on his boot heels,
And clanked 'em like musical bell peals,
He kicked up so high,
He caught his own thigh—
Now he knows how his suffering horse feels.

A cowboy on Saturday night
Wore jeans most immodestly tight.
His steps became mincing,
His groans most convincing,
And teen-agers swooned at the sight.

Pointy-toed boots are the rage
For galloping over the sage,
Or dancing, or walking
Or sitting and talking...
And boots don't wear out; they just age.

ROPING 'N BRANDING

Clyde was a roper of style,
He twirled with finesse and a smile;
He took all his bows,
But forgot about cows,
And his lariat missed by a mile.

A lariat, often, they say,
When practiced with day after day,
Can catch lots of critters
And give them the jitters,
But causes one's arm to decay.

With a branding iron hot from the fire
The cowboy tripped over a wire.
He plumb missed the calf
And hit poor old Alf,
Who jumped over the moon, only higher.

To brand, you take an iron bar
And heat it red hot in the far,
You throw down a calf
And then with a laugh,
You singe his pore little rar.

SHOEING 'N CHEWING

Shoeing a horse can be bruising,
The cowboy's in danger of losing;
A kick near the thigh
Will send him sky high—
A flight that he won't find amusing.

Cowboys love chewin' and spittin'
And action like fightin' and hittin'.
In numerous cases
They'll go into places
Just to act in a way that ain't fittin'.

Always stand upwind from a chewer
And stains on your clothes will be fewer.
Cause when snoose comes your way
It threatens to spray,
And can polka-dot most of the viewer.

One time when spittoons were outmoded,
A cowboy on snoose overloaded;
His cheeks grew in size
And bugged out his eyes
And later, I hear, he exploded.

A snoose chewer needed to spit
So he looked right and left for a pit;
When he sighted a bug,
He shifted his plug
And scored a magnificent hit.

GREENHORNS 'N GRUB

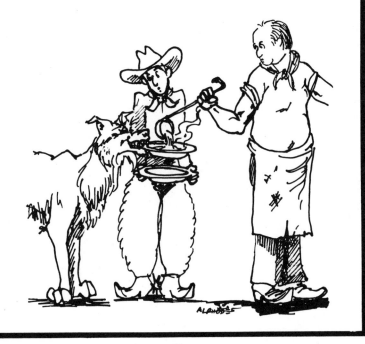

TENDERFOOT TESTAMENTS

Said the city dude, "Don't think me too silly
To follow this path fairly loosily
Endeavoring not
To step on a spot
Where a cow has preceded me juicily!"

A tenderfoot known as Maxine
Thought she knew how to give some vaccine.
She shoved the sharp point
In the little calf's joint
And had hoof-in-the-mouth when last seen.

A greenhorn just trying out snoose
Forgot about packing it loose.
It drooled past his lips,
Clear up to his hips,
And finally he drowned in the juice.

The greenhorn went out on a roundup
To learn all the skills from the ground up,
But thieves got the word
And captured the herd,
And left him abandoned and bound up.

A greenhorn inclined to a quarrel
Crawled up the wrong side of her sorrel;
The horse went all kinky
And tickled her dinky...
Which makes this whole limerick immoral.

A spinster from East in the nation
Saved up for a dude ranch vacation,
But a rhinestone-type cowboy
Found out she knew how, boy,
So she never left Grand Central Station.

VIANDS AND VICTUALS

Cowboys like coffee that's black
And sturdy enough to attack.
They brew it and brew it
Until they can chew it—
It tastes just like tar and shellac.

Oh, a diet of biscuits and beans
Can become an explosive of means,
And that may be why
When old cowboys die,
They find only tatters of jeans.

In spring, in a ranching society,
The ranchers cut calves with propriety,
And then folks are fed
At a bountiful spread
Of oysters—the mountain variety.

A cowboy can put away grub
As though he were built like a tub,
But he's thin as a rail
As he rides down the trail,
And the cook is the one they call "Chub."

"Oh, good," said the dumb little chickens,
"We hear we're the very best pickin's."
But when they were chosen
They ended up frozen,
And later became finger-lickin's.

The ranchwoman got out her jars,
And peeled and pickled for hours,
Which made her so tired
She thought she'd expired,
But revived after nine whiskey sours.

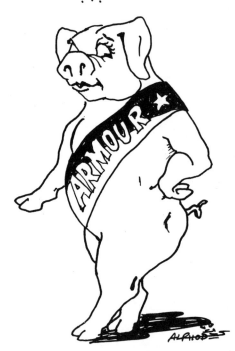

The pig was an absolute charmer;
She used all her wiles on the farmer,
But he's keeping books,
So, in spite of her looks,
She now wears a wrap labeled Armour.

There once was a milk cow whose udder
Dragged on the ground in the mudder,
And some of that ilk
So flavored the milk
That drinking it made us all shudder.

The people who dearly love chicken soup
Have probably not cleaned a chicken coop.
Do you think they would savor it
It they knew their favorite
Was started among all that chicken poop?

Cowboys get up before dawn,
With many a curse and a yawn;
They eat plumb half-hearted,
And wait to get started
A day they now claim is half gone.

INDEX OF FIRST LINES

The big irrigator went wham! 35
The boys in the bunkhouse play gin 50
The brockle-faced cow had a fit 25
The cowboy shook out a big loop 9
The cowboy went shyly a-courting 41
The cowboy wore jeans very tight 54
The cowboy wore spurs on his boot heels, 54
The cowgirl who's out on the tractor 6
The cowpoke a wife did acquire, 48
The coyote said, "Ain't I cute?" 33
The greenhorn went out on a roundup 63
The hay hand fell off of his stack 6
The lodgings of cowboys are humble, 15
The people who dearly love chicken soup 69
The pig was an absolute charmer; 68
The prairie dog pops from his burrow 37
The ranchwoman got out her jars, 68
There once was a milk cow whose udder 69
There once was an albino donkey 30
There was an old sow in the barn 19
The sow toppled over the cream, 18
The view from the outhouse was dandy, 22
Though little in life is for sure, 15
To brand, you take an iron bar 58
To hear some range-riders talk, 10

When Clyde hunkered down on his heels, 13
When riding a bucker take pains 12
While rocking along at a lope 13
With a branding iron hot from the fire 58

Loping the Limerick Trail

Words by Gwen Petersen

Music by Dave Roys

About the Authors...

Jeane and Gwen didn't start out to write a book of limericks. What they started out to do was to take a long automobile trip. What do two writers do cooped up in a small car for hours? They write. It occurred to them that they had never seen a book of limericks about the West as they knew it, so they undertook to correct the deficiency.

Gwen, an honest-to-God ranchperson with horses, cows, sheep, pigs, and chickens, has three books published: *The Ranch Woman's Manual, The Greenhorn's Guide to the Woolly West,* and *Pioneers in Yellowstone: The Story of the Hamilton Stores in Yellowstone National Park.*

Jeane, from the mining-camp side of the state, has a newspaper background and has both written and edited for years, even while counseling and teaching art in high school.

For illustrations, they called on Alan Rhodes, a metallurgical engineer in Tucson, Arizona. Alan partly paid for his engineering degree by illustrating books and lectures for his professors. Since then he divides his art work between producing accurate technical illustrations for engineering manuals and sketching informal portraits of his co-workers—or creating characters for books of limericks.

Jeane and her husband live in Whitefish, Montana. Gwen and her spouse live near Big Timber, Montana.